OUT OF
THE BLOCKS

*Starting strong in the
race of life.*

SEAN KOUPLEN

ISBN: 1-4196-8828-6
ISBN-13: 9781419688287

Visit www.booksurge.com to order additional copies.

To my beautiful wife
and best friend Angela.

You have always supported
me in everything I have tried.

Marrying you is the best
decision I have ever made.

Advanced Praise for **Out of the Blocks**

Students, professors and business leaders everywhere are falling in love with *Out of the Blocks!*

"A must-read for all graduating college seniors. The heartwarming parable is filled with relevant, real-world advice for today's students and recent graduates. I will recommend it to all of my students and new employees!"

—Dr. Steve Greene, COO, Camille's Sidewalk Café and Oral Roberts University Professor

"No one is more qualified to advise graduating students than Sean Kouplen. His accomplishments since graduating from Oklahoma State University are nothing short of remarkable."

—Dr. Jerry Gill, CEO, Oklahoma State University Alumni Association

"Graduating from college is a scary time of uncertainty and change. *Out of the Blocks* is a how-to guide for chartering these turbulent waters."

—Dr. Mary Jane Bias, District 5 Administrator of the Year, State of Oklahoma

"I really enjoyed Out of the Blocks! The story is easy to read, yet contains countless tips for success in the real world, no matter your profession. It really is a must-read for all young professionals."

—Shanna Gomez, Teacher

Add your review today! Just e-mail us at <u>reviews@ outoftheblocks.net</u>.

CONTENTS

Preface

Students throughout the world, both young and old, are terrified about their future. They have succeeded in high school or college, but suddenly graduation is looming and their mind is filled with questions:

How do I choose the best career for me? How do I select the best employer? How do I gain an advantage over my competition in the job search? What is life really like in the corporate world? How can I move up the corporate ladder faster? What are the keys to living a fulfilling life?

Out of the Blocks will help you answer these important questions. It is the story of college student

Jamie Walker and his search for a fulfilling career and life. Along the way, he learns 12 important life lessons that will help guide you in this race called life.

Introduction

My grandfather once told me a story about a man named John who loved to fish.

One sunny spring day, John was fishing on a beautiful pond when he was approached by a childhood friend named Mark. Mark was a successful executive with a local technology company.

"John, you are such a smart guy. Why don't you apply for a job with our company?"

"Why would I want to do that, Mark?"

"If you accept a job with our company and do a good job, in a few years you could work your way into management."

"Why would I want to do that?"

"Once you're a member of management, if you do a good job, in a few years you could work your way up into an executive position."

"Why would I want to do that?"

"Once you are in an executive position, if you do a good job, in a few years you could qualify for stock options and a retirement plan."

"Why would I want to do that?"

"Once you qualify for stock options and a retirement plan, in a few years you could afford to retire."

"Why would I want to do that?"

"Once you retire, you can do the things you really love to do."

"Mark, I'm already doing the thing I love to do."

I admit this story is a little simplistic. Fishing every day with no income makes it difficult to meet our obligations and send our kids to college. It takes revenue to live in this world.

The lesson in my grandfather's story, however, was very important. If you find a career that you enjoy, every day will feel like you are fishing on that beautiful pond. As my grandfather used to say, 'the right job shouldn't feel like a job at all.'

If you settle for a career that you don't enjoy, you will labor through the best years of your life, when you are the healthiest and strongest, waiting for the 'fishing trip' called retirement that may never happen at all.

My goal in writing *Out of the Blocks* is to help you create a career and life that fulfills all your hopes and dreams. By mastering certain skills and processes, you can balance an enjoyable, successful career with a rewarding personal life. You can live comfortably while still meeting your financial obligations and preparing for retirement. You can start strong and finish well in this race called life.

Let's see how Jamie Walker did it.

Reality Check

Leaves crackled under Jamie Walker's feet as he walked home from his last class of the week. The Illinois Technical University Panthers were about to host a huge homecoming game against their instate rival, the University of Illinois, and the campus was buzzing with excitement.

Unfortunately, the football game was the last thing on Jamie's mind. Jamie was worried and confused as he walked down the long sidewalk from the Business Communications building to his apartment.

Jamie only had one semester of college remaining and he just couldn't decide on a career. He had changed majors four times and nothing clicked. Was there something wrong with him? Should he go straight to graduate school or should he work first? If he entered the workforce, where should he work? What industry should he enter and, once he chose an industry, what company should he work for?

The more Jamie thought about his future, the more overwhelmed he became.

Setting the Stage

Jamie Walker attended a small public school system in central Illinois. He wasn't a great student, but he worked hard and was well-liked by his classmates and teachers. Because of his charismatic personality and work ethic, Jamie was voted Most Likely to Succeed by his classmates.

Jamie was the first person in his family to attend college. His father started selling cars immediately after high school and rose through the ranks to purchase the local automobile dealership. Jamie's mother grew up on a small farm north of town and married his father when she was very young. She dedicated her life to being a good mother and wife, and she succeeded at both.

Jamie decided to attend Illinois Technical University because of its great reputation and close proximity to his home, and he never regretted his decision. In fact, he enjoyed his freshman year a little too much. The increased rigor of his coursework and his newfound freedom combined to cause a significant drop in Jamie's grade point. He got back on track his sophomore year and finished strong, but still ended up with a grade point average near the middle of his graduating class.

Jamie built a decent college resume. He was very involved in campus and had been elected to several leadership positions. He worked hard and developed a reputation for being someone you could always depend on.

Throughout his college career, Jamie had been very clear about his direction. If he made good grades and stayed involved on campus, things seemed to take care of themselves. Now, Jamie's future wasn't so clear.

Jamie had put off thoughts and plans about his future for two years and he was now running out of time. He only had two semesters to find the perfect job and he didn't even know where to begin.

Even worse, it seemed like everyone else knew exactly what they were going to do upon graduation. Jamie's best friend Christian was going to law school just like his dad. Mark always knew he was going to be a doctor. Emily fell in love with a pharmaceutical company during her internship there.

Frustrated, Jamie walked into his room and threw down his backpack. He collapsed on his bed and stared at the ceiling. His first few years out of college could set his direction forever.

What was he going to do with the rest of his life?

Wise Counsel

Dr. Jim Carter had been Jamie's academic advisor since he arrived at ITU. Dr. Carter was widely known as one of the best advisors on campus because of his genuine interest in his student's well-being and his relevant, helpful advice. Jamie set up an appointment to see Dr. Carter the following afternoon.

When Jamie arrived, Dr. Carter was just finishing up a phone call. "Come in Jamie. How's my favorite student?" Jamie loved Dr. Carter. He knew Dr. Carter told everyone they were his favorite student, but he didn't care. Jamie never doubted Dr. Carter truly cared for him on a personal level.

"Dr. Carter, I need your help. You know I've worked really hard during my time here at ITU and always tried to do my best. Unfortunately, I only have eight months until graduation and I have absolutely no idea what I am going to do with my life. I've changed my major four times and I just can't seem to decide what I want to do when I graduate. What am I going to do?"

Dr. Carter leaned back in his chair and smiled. He had experienced this conversation hundreds of times during his tenure at ITU. "Jamie, the first thing you need to do is relax. Graduation is a complicated and scary time for everyone and what you're feeling is very normal.

Did you know that in some countries, an individual's aptitude and career direction is determined by the government very early in their life? In other countries, a child must automatically follow in the footsteps of his or her parents. In the United States, we have the freedom to determine our own direction. This is a wonderful opportunity, but it is also very stressful. Determining your career is certainly one of the more important decisions you'll ever make in your life.

Students begin their career path in a variety of ways. Sometimes students have known their career since grade school and sometimes it takes them multiple jobs to figure out what they want to do. Perhaps they follow in a parent's footsteps and emulate his or her career. Maybe they prefer to attend graduate school and try to specialize in a certain field. Sometimes an internship has opened their eyes to possibilities within a company or career field and they follow that path. Often, students just aren't really sure what they want to do. They keep thinking that something will surface and it hasn't yet."

Jamie could definitely relate. "That certainly sounds like me Dr. Carter. My father's business just doesn't have the revenue to support us both and, even if it did, I saw the tension that existed between my father and grandfather when they worked together. I don't want my relationship with my Dad to be like that. Joining the family business just isn't an option for me, but I haven't found any other careers that seem to fit."

Suddenly, Dr. Carter remembered a very similar conversation he experienced about 15 years earlier with a student much like Jamie. "Jamie, I have a good friend and former student that you should meet. Steve Patrick is a local banker here in town who experienced a very similar dilemma when he graduated from ITU. He has done very well in his profession and I think it might be a good idea for the two of you spend some time together. Would you like for me to set up a meeting with you and Steve?"

Jamie had heard of Steve Patrick. He was one of ITU's most beloved young alumni. "Dr. Carter, I would love to meet Mr. Patrick. Thank you so much!"

Jamie left Dr. Carter's office with a glimmer of hope about his future. Maybe Steve Patrick could help him get on the right track.

The Mentor

Jamie was full of anticipation as he walked in the front doors of Premier Bank in Peoria. The bank was one of Illinois' oldest and most distinguished, and definitely looked the part. Jamie approached the receptionist and asked her for directions to Steve Patrick's office. He was directed to the 3rd floor where Premier Bank's executive suites were located.

As he stepped off the elevator, he was approached by a very pleasant woman with her right arm stretched toward him. "Hello Jamie. I'm Laura, Mr. Patrick's assistant. He is in a meeting at the current time, but he is expecting you. Please have a seat and he'll be with you in just a moment."

Steve Patrick had achieved a remarkable number of accomplishments since his graduation from ITU only fifteen years earlier. He was the President of Premier Bank and a very influential member of the Peoria business community. He held leadership positions with the Chamber of Commerce, Rotary Club and ITU Alumni Association, among many other organizations. He had been named ITU's Young Alumni of the Year and Peoria's Business Leader of the Year. Steve had a reputation as a can-do executive who always looked at all sides of an issue. Jamie anxiously awaited their meeting.

In just a few minutes, a nicely tailored man emerged from the office to greet Jamie. He was wearing a gray pin-striped suit with a white shirt and a red tie. His hair was short and slightly spiked with small streaks of gray on the side. He appeared to be in his early to mid 40's, much younger than most bank presidents Jamie knew.

Steve stuck out his hand and introduced himself. "Jamie, my name is Steve Patrick."

Steve Patrick needed no introduction. His picture was plastered all over every alumni publication and billboard in town. "It's a pleasure to meet you, Mr. Patrick. Thank you so much for taking the time to visit with me."

"Jamie, please call me Steve. Mr. Patrick sounds like my dad!"

Steve asked his assistant to hold his calls as the two made their way into his office. Steve had a beautiful corner office with a wonderful view of the river and a park below. He invited Jamie to have a seat at his conference table.

Jamie couldn't help but notice the various awards lining Jamie's walls and shelves. Suddenly he began to feel inadequate and guilty for taking up Steve's time.

Steve noticed Jamie staring at his awards and smiled. "Jamie, don't place too much emphasis on things you can hang on your wall or mantle. As you know, when you do the right things for the right reasons, everything else takes care of itself. Awards are okay, but making a difference is where the real fulfillment is achieved."

Steve asked Jamie if he'd like a bottled water and began their meeting. "Dr. Carter tells me that we have a lot in common. Tell me about yourself."

Jamie shared a brief version of his life growing up in a small town, his father's family business, his decision to join ITU and his wonderful experience there. He also shared his confusion about his future now that graduation was approaching.

Steve could relate to Jamie's story. "Jamie, we do have similar backgrounds. I grew up on a farm in rural Kansas with very little exposure to the outside world. I helped my dad most summers and served as fraternity Rush Chairman for one, so I was also really clueless when it came time to graduate."

"So, how did you end up in banking?" Jamie was very interested in how Steve made his career decision.

"It's really an interesting story. For some reason, our former university president, Dr. John Miller, took an interest in me and introduced me to a good friend of his who owned a bank in the Chicago area. After a couple of meetings with him, I realized that this could be a career I would enjoy. I went to work as an intern for his bank and, fifteen years later, here I am."

Jamie wished that a big break like that would come his way. He had considered so many careers - medicine, law, education, sales – and none of them seemed to be the right fit for him.

Steve continued, noting the concern in Jamie's face. "I was very fortunate, Jamie. Not everyone has the same opportunity that I had. I am convinced, however, that you don't need 'lucky breaks' to get ahead. I believe that we make our own luck."

"What do you mean?"

"Jamie, until now, your life has been a series of semester-long sprints. Each semester since junior high, you have started with a new class schedule, new extracurricular activities, and a clean slate with new teachers. For the last 16 years, you've entered an entirely new world each semester.

The real world isn't like that. It's a marathon and not a sprint. Statistically, you are only one-fourth of the way through your life, so you have many years to make your mark and achieve your dreams.

I know successful people in many different industries and environments. Some started near the top and some started at the bottom, but they all ultimately achieved their goals. With a strong work ethic, persistence, and a positive attitude, you can be successful no matter where you start or what barriers you face. So, don't put so much pressure on yourself when selecting your first job. You have plenty of time to make adjustments if your first career decision isn't right for you."

Jamie listened intently to what Steve was saying. He never really thought about life this way before. He felt so much pressure to make the perfect job decision coming out of college, always feeling that there was a right and a wrong answer.

Steve continued. "Jamie, I know this is a stressful time for you. I have learned a lot since my time as an undergraduate at ITU and I would love to help you avoid some of the mistakes I made along the way. I've also been fortunate to make some great decisions and I would happily share those with you as well. If you have the time, I think I can help you get on the right track."

Jamie was shocked by Steve's willingness to help. "Steve, I would love nothing more. Just name the time and the place!"

"Okay. Why don't we plan on meeting once a month for awhile? We will discuss a different topic at each of our meetings, nothing too structured. Then you can work on that topic until we meet again."

"That sounds perfect Steve. Thank you very much."

"Unfortunately, we're out of time today", apologized Steve. "I have a lunch meeting to attend, but why don't we get together next month to review the first life lesson?"

"That sounds great. Steve, I know you're busy. Are you sure you don't mind spending this much time with me?"

Steve laughed. "I don't know where I would be if Dr. Carter and Dr. Miller hadn't show an interest in me. This is the least I can do. Just promise me that you'll return the favor for someone else someday."

"I certainly will."

The Five Advancement Skills

There was snow on the ground as Jamie walked down University Avenue for his first monthly meeting with Steve.

Steve was walking across the bank lobby as Jamie entered the front door. "Good afternoon, Jamie! Let me say hello to one of my clients and I will meet you upstairs in just a couple of minutes."

After a quick visit about the ITU football team and the latest university happenings, Steve was ready to jump in. "Jamie, I realize that you are just beginning your job search and your main concern right now is to land a good job with a good company. I think it would be valuable, however, for me to spend a little time helping you to understand what it takes to be successful in the business world. Does that sound okay?"

"Sure it does, Steve."

"Jamie, what is your primary professional goal?"

Jamie had never been shy about his ambition. "Well Steve, I am hoping to find a great job that will grow into a managerial or executive position as soon as possible."

"That's exactly what I thought you would say, because that is exactly what I thought when I graduated from college. Jamie, contrary to popular belief, you probably will not, and should not, be named CEO of your new company on day one. In reality, your next five to ten years should be spent developing a few critical skills that you will need to contribute at a high-level to your organization. So, we're going to spend some time today talking about how to be a top performer in the real world."

Jamie was excited. He rarely received 'real world' advice during his academic career.

"Jamie, one of the most surprising things I have learned during my career is that you just can't bluff your way through life. Magazines teach us how to make ourselves look successful. They tell us how to dress, what to drive, and even how to 'kiss up' to the boss. Unfortunately, these things will only work temporarily.

You must create value to move up within any organization or to successfully own your own business. You must truly love what you do and not just go through the motions. You must be technically proficient in your job.

I also believe, however that you must also develop five critical skills to be successful and advance to the top of your organization. I call them the five advancement skills."

"What are these advancement skills?" Jamie was anxious to get started.

"Jamie, I believe the first essential skill for a great leader is excellent time management. I know you are busy now, but you cannot imagine the pace of your life after you become a manager or executive. You must balance a busy family life that includes quality time with your spouse and kids, school activities, church activities, birthday parties, and much more with a professional life that includes day-to-day management and employee issues, community involvement, investor relations, client relations and other important duties.

This is a very difficult balancing act. I have many friends who made it to the top of their organization, or built their own business, only to lose their wife and children because they took them for granted. I have other friends that spent so much time doing personal business at work, their businesses suffered and they are no longer employed. As an executive, you have to set the tone for the entire organization without sacrificing your family life. As you can see, time management and prioritization are essential to your future success."

Jamie thought he had been busy at ITU, but it sounded like he was just scratching the surface of Steve's busy life.

Steve continued. "Jamie, our second critical skill is the ability to effectively communicate with others. You can have the best ideas in the world, but it won't matter if you can't communicate them to others in a verbal or written manner.

Interestingly, communication skills have proven to be the number one predictor of executive success.

As you know, communication includes reading, writing, listening and speaking. By the way, which of these do you think is most important?"

"Speaking. I always see Fortune 500 CEO's giving speeches in their annual meetings and on various talk shows and they are so polished."

Steve was amused by Jamie's answer. "That's what I always thought, but listening is actually proven to be, far and away, the most important communication skill. Employees, clients, investors and peers want to be heard. Leaders who thoughtfully listen to their stakeholders and follow through on their commitments tend to develop a very large circle of influence."

"Great advice. What are the other critical skills?"
"Jamie, I believe that emotional intelligence is the third critical skill. The ability to sense others' feelings and concerns, and respond appropriately to them is a rare talent that really separates great managers from good managers. Employees must believe that you truly care about them and their well-being, not just about yourself and your goals.

Some people have amazing analytical skills and industry knowledge, but they just can't seem to get along with those around them. This is a career killer and is often due to a lack of emotional intelligence."

"I can definitely see emotional intelligence being a critical skill." Jamie was really enjoying this discussion with Steve.

"Jamie, our fourth critical skill is the ability to develop and maintain relationships, commonly known as networking.

Your success going forward will largely depend on your relationships and reputation. You've always heard that 'it's who you know and not what you know' that matters. Unfortunately, that's only partly true. It's who you know *and* what they think of you that counts. I know many people that I would never hire because they just have not proven that they can get the job done.

Many times, when people hear the word 'networking', they think it means attending parties or events and handing out business cards. This is a small part of networking. Meeting people is certainly important, but networking is more about what you do after you meet an individual.

Great networkers make a great living, and a great life, out of helping others. They have this innate ability to bring people together to benefit everyone involved. Over time, people begin to view them as a resource and someone who truly cares about their well-being, and this is a powerful position to hold."

"Wow. I always thought networking sounded kind of fake and insincere, but what you're talking about is just the opposite."

"That's exactly right. Networking is just caring about people and trying to help them. The more you help others to be successful, the more successful you will become."

"That's a great point Steve. What is the last critical skill?" Jamie was disappointed that today's visit was coming to an end.

"Jamie, the final skill is the most important skill, but it is also the most difficult. It is the ability to develop and maintain trust with others."

That sounded pretty simple to Jamie. "I don't understand, Steve. Being trustworthy sounds pretty straightforward to me. Just tell the truth."

"I know it sounds simple, Jamie, but it's harder than you might realize. While right and wrong is pretty black and white as a student, it's not always so clear in the business world. Let me give you some examples.

You take credit for one of your peer's work by merely staying quiet and accepting the praise. You convince your board of directors to make a strategic move by omitting certain information from your presentation. You charge one of your best clients an unfair fee just because you know they are loyal to you and will not leave. You pad your expense report by adding lunches that were really only social in nature. You promise to follow up on issues that you know are important to your employees, but you never do. You take a large bonus even when the company is not performing well. Are you getting the picture Jamie?"

"I am. None of your examples are black and white, but I can see how they could definitely damage your credibility."

"That's exactly right. These situations don't involve outright lying, cheating or stealing, but they all lead to deterioration in trust. Unfortunately, often times, these wrongdoings just slide by and are never even brought to the attention of the individual who did them. They are discussed by peers or subordinates behind closed doors, but never with the person that committed the transgression. Your effectiveness as a leader just diminishes over time and you don't even know why."

"Why wouldn't your peers or subordinates confront you about their issues, Steve?"

"Jamie, in the real world, people need income and security for their families. They're often afraid to do anything that will jeopardize their employment, so they stay quiet when they shouldn't. The right corporate culture encourages this type of feedback and protects those employees who have the courage to share their feelings, but these types of organizations are extremely rare.

So, as a manager or executive, you must be above reproach and think about the consequences of your actions each and every day. Your coworkers and employees must know that they can trust you under any circumstance, and that you will always look out for their best interest. Your reputation is truly the most important asset you will ever own.

"That's really interesting. I always thought that moving up the ladder meant outperforming everyone else, but there's much more to being a great leader than just performance."

"That's right Jamie. Fortunately, the five skills I mentioned will benefit you no matter what career you choose. So, the sooner you develop these skills, the sooner you will be ready to lead others. Unfortunately, many people are thrust into leadership roles before they have developed these skills and this can lead to disaster.

During your first 5 to 10 years out of school, your primary professional goal should be to develop these skills, not to rapidly move up the corporate ladder. So, as you are considering your career and the first company where you will work, think about where you can best develop these skills."

"That makes a lot of sense Steve. This really changes my perspective on how to choose my first place of employment. Do you think the leadership positions I've held in high school and college have helped me to develop these skills?"

"Extracurricular activities in high school and college certainly accelerate your development of these skills. However, keep in mind that you are typically leading groups for a very short period of time, usually a semester or two at the most. And, most of the time, you have had a faculty advisor or sponsor to help make sure you were successful. This is very different than leading a department or company.

Your leadership of a department or company could last for years or decades. This extended timeframe creates some inherent challenges that you typically don't experience in extracurricular organizations. Plus, you are largely on your own. You have a Board of Directors to give you strategic input, but it is your job to handle daily operational challenges and produce results.

Jamie, let's think about today's discussion and next time, we'll talk about how to prepare for your future employer so that you will have an edge over your competition."

As Jamie walked out of Steve's office, he realized that he had a lot to learn before he would be prepared to lead a team or an organization. Strangely, he felt comfort in the fact that during his initial years out of college, he should focus on preparing key skills and not try to be CEO overnight.

Life Lesson #1

You can't bluff your way through life. To excel professionally, you must add value to your organization and your clients.

To be a successful leader, you must develop five key skills: Time management, communications, emotional intelligence, networking and trustworthiness.

Preparation

Christmas lights shone brightly throughout the business district as Jamie approached the front door of Premier Bank for his second monthly meeting with Steve. Jamie had just completed his last final and was excited about visiting with Mr. Patrick before his drive home for the holidays.

Arriving 10 minutes early for his appointment, Jamie was promptly greeted by Laura. "Jamie, Steve is just wrapping up a phone call, but he'll be with you shortly."

Steve soon arrived, upbeat and friendly, as usual. "Good afternoon, Jamie. How were finals?"

"Not bad. Calculus was a little rough, but the others were manageable. I should be able to escape with pretty good grades this semester."

"That's great Jamie. There's no better feeling than completing finals.

Before you head home, let's get you on the right track with your first job choice. My notes show that we are going to talk about our second life lesson – Preparation."

Jamie wrote the word 'preparation' down in his notebook. He didn't want to be negative, but this seemed to be a pretty bland topic. Jamie prided himself on being prepared for any task he faced.

Steve continued. "Jamie, what do you know about me?"

Jamie was caught off guard by Steve's question. He recounted the information that Dr. Carter had shared about Steve and a few facts Jamie had learned while reading various alumni magazines.

"Do you know my wife's name?"

"No sir."

"What about my children's names? What do I like to do for fun? What do I look for in a potential employee? What am I like as a boss?"

"I don't know any of those things, Steve." Suddenly, Jamie didn't feel so prepared.

Steve was making progress. "Jamie, have you ever played competitive sports?"

"Yes sir."
In fact, Steve knew that Jamie was a good athlete in high school. "Jamie, think about how you would prepare for playing key rivals. First, you focused on preparing yourself. You had to be in top physical condition. You had to know the plays. You had to be mentally prepared. You had to make sure that your skills were as fine tuned as they could be so that you would play your best in every game. Correct?"

"Absolutely."

"If you think about it, however, that was only half of the battle. You also had to focus on your opponent, didn't you? It didn't do much good to spend hours in the weight room and running bleachers if your opponent ran an offense or defense that your team couldn't figure out."

Jamie agreed. "This is true. I distinctly remember two games in which we were defeated by inferior opponents simply because they had a better game plan than we did."

"Exactly. They knew more about you than you knew about them. They knew your tendencies, strengths and weaknesses, and how to use them to their advantage. That's what I mean by preparation."

Jamie loved sports analogies, but he didn't quite understand how this applied to his situation. "I understand what you're saying Steve, but I'm not quite sure how this applies to me."

"It's simple, Jamie. I know much more about you than you know about me. I know that you are a hard worker with great interpersonal skills. I also know that you're not real crazy about details and prefer to delegate those to someone else."

Jamie was impressed. How could Steve know all of this?

"You mentioned working for your dad's business. I know that he owns an auto dealership in your hometown. You have a wonderful family who is very supportive of you. Since working at the auto dealership is all you and your family have ever done, you need some help finding your way."

Remarkable! In two minutes, Steve had literally pegged him perfectly.

"I made a couple of calls to prepare for our meeting," explained Steve. "I didn't want to waste both of our time by making recommendations that didn't fit you."

Suddenly Jamie understood why Steve had the reputation of being such an amazing business developer. Who wouldn't want to buy from him? If he prepared half this much for his sales calls, he would absolutely blow away his competition.

"Jamie, you have done a great job preparing yourself up to this point. There is no substitute for your hard work in high school and college, but you need to take your preparation to the next level."

Steve knew Jamie was talented, but this just wasn't enough. "Jamie, preparing yourself with a great resume, good interview skills and a nice suit is only half of the battle. Just like you prepared for your high school football competition by watching hours and hours of tape to learn their tendencies, you must now learn to prepare for your target in the real world."

"But who is my target?" asked Jamie.

"Your target is anyone you are trying to persuade or defeat", Steve explained. "In my business, this can include a potential employee, client, vendor or competitor. In your situation, you need to persuade a potential employer that they simply cannot live without you. So, how would you prepare for them?"

Jamie was beginning to understand. "I would learn as much about them as possible. Things like their history, plans for the future, culture, likes and dislikes, and competitors."

"Great start. You would also want to find out information about your potential supervisor, or the person making the hiring decision. What type of person is she? Does she surround herself with people that compliment or mirror her? What are some of the challenges and opportunities that she faces?

Additionally, you must determine whether the company is right for you. Does their culture and core values fit with yours? Is there opportunity for advancement if you excel in your work? Where does the company see itself in 5, 10 or 20 years? Is the company you are considering an acquisition target or are they planning to expand? Remember, your primary goal is to develop the key skills we discussed last month. Will this company help you do that?

You also need to know about the industry in which the company operates. Is it expanding or contracting? Is there a lot of industry consolidation or shifting of operations overseas?

All of these things are easier to find than you might think. Much of the information is available online and in company promotional materials. You can also ask your advisor, career placement services and your alumni association for the name of alumni currently working at the company. You'll be amazed how much ITU alumni will help you if you just ask!"

Jamie understood exactly what Steve was saying. It wasn't enough to show up to a job interview. He had to know more about the company than they knew about themselves.

Laura popped her head in with a reminder for Steve. "Steve, don't forget about your meeting."

"Jamie, I hate to run, but I have a meeting downtown in about 30 minutes. Why don't you work with Laura to set an appointment for mid-January? We'll talk about our third life lesson then."

"Sounds great Steve. I hope you and your family have a wonderful holiday season."

"You too, Jamie. Merry Christmas!"

On his way back to the car, Jamie thought about the great advice Steve had given him. He did not realize that preparation could be such an amazing differentiator. These monthly meetings could really be beneficial for Jamie's future.

Life Lesson #2

*Preparation tops talent
every time.*

*Preparation means not only
performing at your best,
but also knowing your
target better than they know
themselves.*

Focus

Jamie had a wonderful Christmas break with his family. He told his Dad about his visits with Steve Patrick and all that he was learning. Jamie's father never attended college and always worked in the car business, so he listened intently as Jamie talked about choosing a career. He was thrilled that Jamie found a mentor to guide him.

After Christmas break ended, Jamie drove back to Peoria for his next meeting with Steve. As he walked into the lobby of Premier Bank, Jamie wondered what today's life lesson would be.

"Good morning, Jamie. Happy New Year!" Laura always greeted him so warmly. "Come on in, Steve can see you now."
"Hello, Jamie. How was your Christmas break?"

Jamie and Steve exchanged pleasantries about how much they both enjoyed the holiday season. Then, it was down to business.

"Jamie, today we're going to talk about focus. I believe that focus will be the single greatest factor in your personal and professional success."

The single greatest factor? That's a pretty strong statement. Jamie was definitely listening.

Steve continued. "Jamie, the vast majority of our population just exists day to day. There's no real purpose in their lives and they just go through the motions. I did this for many years until I received a wake up call one day in college.

I really struggled my freshman year. I came to ITU from a small town without any real purpose. My parents wanted me to go to college, so I went. Unfortunately, I was unmotivated and rarely went to class. I almost flunked out."

Jamie was shocked. "Steve, I just assumed that everything had always come easy for you."
"Quite the contrary. I really started out behind the eight ball. Fortunately, early in my sophomore year, I developed a lifelong friendship

with a senior named Damon Jackson. Damon was a leader on the ITU campus who seemed to like me.

One evening, he began telling me about the importance of setting personal goals. I always sat goals for myself, but never to the extent that he did. My goals were always general in nature with no specific timeline or accountability.
Damon taught me to visualize my future and to set SMART goals that were specific, measurable, attainable, realistic, and time-sensitive. He believed that 'feel good' goals listing what we hoped to someday achieve were a waste of time. Damon Jackson believed that we take specific actions each and every day to create our own future, and so do I.

He taught me to break every personal goal down into very specific, measurable and time-specific action plans. For example, if I wanted to be student body president, I couldn't just write that down. I would have to develop strategies for how I would get from my current situation to the goal.

In this case, I needed to improve my grades and meet more people by getting involved in my fraternity and college activities. Ultimately, my plan included my running for a College Senator seat within our student government association and finally, running for student body president.

I posted these goals and action plans above my bed, on my bathroom mirror and in my vehicle where I would see them at the beginning and ending of every single day.

This process literally changed my life. I began reviewing these goals and action plans every day and holding myself accountable for their accomplishment.

Over time, I became more focused and productive. My grades improved drastically and I become more involved on campus. Soon, I realized that I had a gift for leading others and the rest, as they say, is history."

"So, you're saying that focus was the key to your success?"

"Yes. I am convinced that the only reason that I moved from the bottom 20% of students at ITU to Student Body President and a Top Ten Senior in only three years was focus. I was more focused than the other students I was competing against. I woke up every day with a very clear purpose and plan. I believe this made all the difference.

This disciplined method of very specific goal-setting and personal accountability has driven me to this very day and it will work for you as well."

"Steve, I appreciate the advice. That's an amazing story."

"Thanks Jamie. Here's my point. The most successful people I know never stop setting goals for themselves. Their goals just get bigger and bigger over time."

"So, how does this apply to my career search, Steve?"
"Making the right career decision is your most important goal and you have taken the first steps by calling your advisor and now meeting with me. Now, your career decision is simply a matter of focus and narrowing your choices. You have to narrow your career options before you can implement a strategy."

"Steve, this is easier said than done. How do I narrow my career choices?"

"Now that you understand the importance of focus, let's wrap up today's meeting with a very challenging homework assignment. I want you to do some serious soul searching over the next month and come back here with the answer to three important questions that I believe will help you to choose your first career.

What do I enjoy?
What are my strengths?
What do I want to accomplish in life?

"Sounds great Steve. This could be a real breakthrough for me. Thank you."

Jamie said goodbye to Steve and headed back to his apartment. Focused goal-setting had such an incredible effect on Steve Patrick's life, just think what it could do for Jamie!

Life Lesson #3

Focus is the single greatest factor in your personal and professional success.

Focus includes visualizing your future, clarifying your goals, developing specific action plans to achieve your goals, and holding yourself accountable each and every day.

Know Yourself

For the next four weeks, Jamie spent at least one hour every night contemplating Steve's three questions. He took personality tests and talked with friends, family and professors about his strengths and weaknesses.

Jamie also spent a considerable amount of time in self-examination, something he had never really done before. What did he really enjoy? What were his strengths? What did he want to accomplish in life?

These questions proved to be very challenging. Jamie was so programmed to choose a career that sounded impressive to his friends and his family, that he had a difficult time focusing on what he truly enjoyed and wanted to accomplish in life. Over time, he finally developed clear answers to Steve's questions.

By the time his next meeting with Steve rolled around, Jamie was ready. Laura showed him into Steve's conference room.

Steve was in a great mood. "Good morning, Jamie. I believe we are going to answer your three critical questions today. Is that correct?"

"Yes sir. I've given this a lot of thought and I have the answers. This was a very difficult, and uncomfortable, exercise. I've never experienced this type of self-analysis, but I learned a lot about myself and I'm really glad you asked me do it."

"That's great Jamie. Let's begin with question one. What do you enjoy?"

"Well, after several stops and starts, I realized that I enjoy many things, but I've narrowed them to my top four.

First, I love leadership. The process of working with a team to create a shared vision is so energizing for me. I also enjoy breaking that vision down into manageable objectives and motivating my teammates to ensure that the objectives are completed in a timely manner.

I also love to build relationships. I've been elected to a number of leadership positions and I was recruited by others to run for virtually all of them. I was also successful selling cars for my dad's dealership and I've done some fundraising for our college. I've been told that I develop credibility and trust very quickly.

I also like numbers. I'm not particularly interested in the details like an accountant or bookkeeper, but I do enjoy analyzing financial trends and looking for efficiency opportunities. I guess you could say that I like 'big picture' numbers.

Finally, I also realized that I need variety. I function most effectively in a fast-paced environment where I have several projects going on at the same time. I don't seem to do as well when things are slow or I have to limit my focus to only one project."

"Well done, Jamie!" Steve was impressed. Obviously, Jamie had given this serious consideration. He was anxious to go further.

"Now, what are your strengths?"

"My strengths, not surprisingly, correlate closely with the things I enjoy. First, I seem to have success in building relationships and developing friendships. I don't really like 'hard selling' and get a little uncomfortable with putting excessive pressure on people. But, I am effective at building trust and educating potential customers.

I am also creative, particularly when it comes to marketing and product development. I've always excelled in my marketing classes and feel like I really have a knack for developing quality marketing plans and strategies.

Finally, I think I'm an effective leader. As I mentioned earlier, I've held several leadership positions and my teams typically exceed expectations. I also think I communicate well and my team member seem to respect my honesty and objectivity."
"Very interesting." Steve couldn't help but notice the similarities between himself and Jamie.

"What are your major weaknesses?"

"I have several, but I'll boil it down to the top three. I'm impatient and not always as thorough as I should be. Sometimes my ability to multi-task can backfire on me and I don't take the time to focus on the details associated with critical decisions.

Also, as I mentioned earlier, I could be better at holding others accountable. I want to be liked and this is sometimes a problem. I'm very good at creating the vision, but I'm not particularly good at holding others accountable for the details.

Finally, to be honest, I also struggle with rejection. I'm very good at educating potential customers about a product. I just don't do well when people reject my sales pitch. I'm a little insecure when it comes to being turned down."

Steve was very pleased, but wanted him to continue.

"Now for the really tough question. What do you want to accomplish in life?"

"Steve, this is a tough one. Since I've never been in the 'real world,' I'm not exactly sure what I want to accomplish. I have, however, seen what I don't want out of life.

A few of my high school friends had high-powered executive fathers who were never around. They drove great cars and wore expensive clothes, but they never seemed to have time for their families. They never came to games or practices, and I would rarely see them at all. I saw their relationships and realize that I don't want to be like that.

I would love to be a community leader who really makes a difference and would love a career that would give me the flexibility to get involved. I want to be successful professionally and provide my family with financial security so we don't have to worry all the time about money. I want to maintain emphasis on my spiritual life since I believe that's why we're all here. Any position that requires me to go against my morals and ethics just won't work for me.

Finally, I want to be a good husband and father. I want to have the time and flexibility to be there for my wife and children when they need my support. More than anything, I want a career that will allow me to achieve this objective."

"This is great work, Jamie. Now, let's take this one step further and use this information to determine which types of careers would fit you the best."

Steve recommended that Jamie take his information to ITU's Career Services Center for further analysis. He called a friend there and set up an appointment for Jamie.

As Jamie left the meeting, he really felt like he was beginning to make progress. He understood the importance of preparation and focus, and how critical it was to choose a career that was consistent with his strengths, joys and life goals.

Life Lesson #4

Choose a career that is consistent with your personal strengths, joys and life goals.

Ask yourself three important questions before choosing a career:

What do I enjoy?
What are my strengths?
What do I want to accomplish in life?

Narrowing the Field

The following week, Jamie arrived at ITU's Career Services Center. The Career Services Center was a very impressive area on the 4th floor of ITU's Student Center. In his preparation for the meeting, he learned that the CSC had many tools for helping students determine the right careers for them. He was really surprised and previously thought the CSC's only function was bringing potential employers to campus.

Jamie's counselor was an impressive middle-aged woman named Sandy Park. Ms. Park retired from a distinguished career as an executive at one of the state's largest oil companies and joined ITU about five years earlier. Jamie's friends said that Sandy was an outstanding counselor who truly understood what it took to succeed in the real world.

"Good afternoon, Jamie. Please come in."

Jamie glanced around Ms. Park's office. It was professionally decorated with awards and certificates on her shelves and walls. He was excited to visit with her.

"What can I do for you today?"

"Ms. Park, I need to narrow my career choices and I could really use your help."

Jamie and Ms. Park spent over an hour reviewing his answers to Steve's three questions. She was impressed with his self-awareness and assured him that together they could target careers that would fit his talents, interests and life goals. Ms. Park gave Jamie one additional questionnaire and asked him to give her office one week to analyze his information.

In just a few days, Ms. Park called Jamie for a follow-up meeting. "Jamie, I have great news for you. It looks like there are several careers that fit your profile." Jamie couldn't wait to hear Ms. Park's recommendations!

"It appears that the top five career choices for you are as follows: Sales Management, Management Consulting, Financial Services, Higher Education, and Public Service.

There isn't any significance in the order. Given your skill sets, it appears that any of these could work well for you."

Jamie was thrilled. For the first time in his life, he actually had a concrete list of possible career options. He visited with Ms. Park about the pros and cons of each of these possibilities. They were all appealing to him in some way.

Jamie then visited with Dr. Carter, his academic advisor, and did some additional research on each of the five options. He was able to narrow his career choices down to three.

First, Jamie eliminated sales management because he felt that to be an effective sales manager, he needed to distinguish himself as a successful sales professional.
He had the same concern about management consulting. How could he teach others to be more efficient or effective when he had never truly held a management role in the real

world? He knew recent graduates who had done well in the consulting field, but he thought a little practical experience would benefit him.

Ultimately, Jamie had narrowed his search to three areas- Financial Services, Higher Education and Public Service. Jamie was looking forward to sharing this information with Steve at their next meeting.

Two weeks passed and Jamie made his way toward Steve's office. As Jamie walked into the lobby of Premier Bank, he was about to burst with excitement. Steve summoned him back to his office.

Jamie summarized his last few weeks for Steve and shared his top three job choices. Steve was excited and wanted to help further.

"Jamie, do you have any experience in any of these fields?"

Jamie admitted his inexperience. "I've been a teaching assistant and I've dealt with bankers and financial planners in our family business. I also know several politicians and staffers, but, I really don't have any first-hand experience in any of these fields."

"Well, we'd better get you some."

"Steve, with all due respect, I only have four months until graduation. That really isn't enough time to launch careers in three completely different industries."

Steve laughed. "I know Jamie, but there are other ways to get practical knowledge about an industry. Let me give you the names and numbers of good friends of mine who have excelled in each of your chosen fields. Just call them to set up an appointment. They'll tell you anything you want to know about their chosen careers.

My grandfather used to tell me, 'If you want to be successful, find someone who's been successful and do what they did.' I've always lived by this advice and I believe it will work for you too."

Steve gave Jamie the names of three close friends of his: a financial planner, a university professor, and a State Senator.

Jamie was very grateful. "Thank you so much Steve. I'll call them all immediately to set up appointments."

"Jamie, I will ask them to give you up to 30 minutes of their time. So, please be prepared and use your time efficiently. Don't forget to ask them absolutely anything. You need to get the real scoop on their careers, not just the 30-second sound byte of why their chosen career is the greatest."

Jamie couldn't believe it was coming down to this. His conversations with these individuals could help set the direction for the rest of his life!

Life Lesson #5

Success is very simple.

Find a mentor who has accomplished what you wish to accomplish.

Then follow your mentor's guidance and do what he or she did.

Due Diligence

Over the next two weeks, Jamie met with all of Steve's friends for thirty-minute meetings. The feedback from these three individuals was eye-opening and extremely valuable.

Jamie's first appointment was with David Parker who, according to Steve, was the top financial planner in the area. Mr. Parker openly shared his professional experience with Jamie.

"Jamie, my father was a mechanic and we always seemed to struggle for money. I recall watching my parents fight over the smallest purchases. Finances always created a great deal of stress in their relationship.

Furthermore, when my grandfather passed away, I watched all of his children fight over his assets because he wasn't clear enough in his will. The federal government ended up getting most of his estate anyway.

I didn't realize it, but I think these experiences had a huge impact on me. I've always wanted to be financially secure and help others achieve financial security as well. It became obvious that financial planning was the perfect career for me."

Jamie was very intrigued by how David's life experiences had shaped his career choice.

"Jamie, becoming a quality financial planner takes time. First, you must educate yourself and achieve very challenging professional designations. This is not easy and many people give up. You must commit to lifelong learning so that you stay sharp on all new industry trends and changes in law.

You must like people *and* numbers. The life of a financial planner is initially about sales and building your client base and later more about managing the finances of your clients.

Eventually, your performance and reputation will drive your business, but in the early days you have to work very hard to build your client base one person at a time. I started calling friends, family and people in the phone book to build my practice and it was extremely challenging. Over time, as my contacts and referral base grew, it got much easier.

Financial planning is a great profession because you can change people's lives. You can help them reach financial goals they never dreamed possible. You can help protect them in case of unexpected personal loss, and you can help to ensure that future generations utilize their inherited assets wisely.

This has been a wonderful career for me because of the tremendous personal and financial freedom that it has provided. My clients are the boss, not a 'superior' who tells me what to do. As long as they are happy and receiving the results they expect, it doesn't matter when I come in, leave, or take vacation.

Finally, the financial rewards are significant. There is no limit to your income potential if you work hard and serve your clients well.

Jamie thanked Mr. Parker for his time. There were obviously tremendous benefits to this type of work.

Jamie's second appointment was with Dr. Sharon Kendall, the Dean of ITU's College of Business. Dr. Kendall was a distinguished professor and administrator and she was beloved by students and faculty alike. She was a brilliant teacher who had a charismatic personality and genuine love for students and alumni.

Dr. Kendall shared her experiences, as well as her rationale for choosing higher education as a career path. "I worked as an accountant in the private sector for five years. I enjoyed it, but it was never my passion. I started taking some MBA classes at night and simply wanted to continue taking classes after I completed the program. My husband was supportive, so we moved to Champaign and I joined the doctoral program at the University of Illinois. This was a major lifestyle change for us and it required tremendous personal sacrifice.

There are several things that you should know about a career in higher education. First, it is a wonderful life. As a professor, you have significant flexibility and stability. You can make a difference in the lives of many people, and you spend your life in a high-energy, youthful environment. You're constantly surrounded by the best and brightest minds in the world. You are paid to learn and teach, and this is a wonderful combination.

It's not all glamour, however. The road to a tenured professorship is very difficult. You earn very little as a doctoral student and the doctoral program is extremely challenging. Upon graduation, you typically need to move to a different city and university from your alma mater to be marketable. There is significant pressure to be published and you have to do an enormous amount of research and writing. Often, people become seduced by the teaching aspect of being a faculty member, but they don't think about the research necessary to be tenured professor.

There is also very little upward mobility. Since universities rarely have large increases in revenue, pay raises are few and far between and opportunities for advancement are rare. You must be motivated by the difference you make in students' lives and not the title on your business card. This is sometimes frustrating for young professors who come into our profession with unrealistic expectations.

Finally, it's important to consider the compensation. Early on, things can get a little frustrating because your classmates are earning two to three times your salary in the private sector. You will catch up over time and, if you're really good, consulting engagements can help you to pass them, but it will take patience.

Jamie thanked Dr. Kendall for her time. He could see definite advantages and disadvantages to a career in higher education.

Jamie's final appointment was with Brad Murphy, an Illinois State Senator. Brad was a graduate of ITU in his early 50's. He was a successful business owner before running for the Senate four years ago. Brad was a likeable, energetic individual who obviously cared about his constituents.

"Jamie, I really never planned to be a politician. Like you, I have always gravitated to leadership positions. I enjoy making a difference and feel like I can in state government.

As you know, I owned my own business for years before running for office. I became passionate about small business issues and became an advocate for them. Ultimately, I was recruited to run for office. Let me assure you, there are significant differences between private business and life as a public official.

In public office, other people's problems become your own. You have to be a great listener with genuine empathy for others. You also have to be patient. The political process is long and difficult, and it often takes years to advance legislation. You can't be frustrated by the bureaucracy and you must respect authority and your place within the process.

Your schedule is also really hectic. You have to attend many evening and weekend meetings and must be accessible to your constituents whenever they need you. A public servant means just that, you are a servant to your public.

Finally, your life is under a microscope. Your friends, family and contributors are all subject to public scrutiny. You must keep your reputation clean and avoid the slightest appearance of impropriety.

The job also has many significant benefits. You can impact the lives of so many people and effect significant societal change. You make tremendous contacts and rub shoulders with difference makers. You also achieve a certain level of name recognition which, if you do a good job, will always be an asset for you. There's a nice retirement package, but the short-term pay definitely leaves something to be desired.

Jamie, whether you're an elected public servant or hold a staff position within government, always remember that serving the public must be your passion. There are higher paying jobs with better hours, but there are very few jobs where you can make such a difference in the lives of so many.

Jamie was impressed with Brad. "Thank you so much, Senator Murphy. I know you're very busy and I appreciate your time."

Jamie learned more in 90 minutes with Steve's friends than he had learned in 22 years of 'guessing' about careers. He was amazed at how helpful people were when you just ask.

Life Lesson #6

Every career has positives and negatives associated with it.

The most important thing is to enjoy what you do every day and feel that you are making a difference.

If you look forward to your career every day, you are successful.

The Decision

After his meetings, Jamie had a great deal to think about. Each of his possible careers choices had significant advantages and disadvantages. Where should he begin? He called Laura for one final meeting with Steve.

"He was expecting your call, Jamie. We realize that you need to start interviewing soon. Can you come by this afternoon?" Jamie was always amazed at Steve's thoughtfulness and attention to detail.

Jamie showed up at Steve's office around 4pm and was promptly greeted by Laura. Soon Steve arrived. "Hey Jamie! I bet we have a lot to talk about. Come on in."
Jamie told Steve all about his conversations with Mr. Parker, Dr. Kendall and Senator Murphy. " Steve,

each of these outstanding individuals was very open about the pros and cons associated with their career. They were all so passionate about what they do and they all make a difference in their own way."

"They are all great people. Did your conversations give you any clarity about your own future?"

"I think so. I have given this a great deal of thought. I love the idea of higher education and public service, but I think it makes sense to spend some time in the 'real world' first.

Dr. Kendall and Senator Murphy both spent some time in the private sector before embarking upon their chosen careers. They both felt that their foundations in business served them well, and I believe it will also serve me well, so I'm leaning toward a career in Financial Services."

"That makes a lot of sense Jamie. Many successful people change careers during their lives. Starting in financial services certainly wouldn't preclude you from entering politics or getting your doctorate later in life."

"Thank you Steve. I really appreciate everything you've done for me."

"Good luck Jamie. I'm sure proud of you. Now, be sure to check in and let me know how your job search is going."

Jamie would never forget what Steve had done for him. His advice and experience had truly changed Jamie's life forever.

Race Day

Armed with his newfound clarity and the terrific advice he had received, Jamie began interviewing with the top financial service companies in the region. He researched the companies extensively and only interviewed with those companies that fit his profile.

He prepared for every interview as if he were preparing for the biggest football game of his life. He knew more about each company than they knew about themselves. When necessary, he would seek out an alumnus who worked there to get to the 'real scoop' about the company. He was better prepared than any of his competitors.

During his job interview, Jamie always looked his best. As Steve suggested, he purchased a quality navy suit, white shirt and a red tie. Jamie always wore black shoes that were polished to perfection. He maintained excellent posture and eye contact, and answered all of the interview questions clearly and concisely. He always asked excellent questions that showed his extensive preparation and knowledge of the company. He followed every interview up with a nice, handwritten note thanking the interviewer for their time and expressing his interest in the company.

In the end, Jamie received job offers from three outstanding financial service firms. This was an amazing accomplishment, given that Jamie's grade point ranked in the middle of his graduating class. Jamie's results certainly validated the strategies that Steve had taught him.

One of the firms would require a significant relocation, so Jamie politely declined. He just could not decide between the final two offers. Both potential employers were local and very well-respected. One offer paid slightly more than the other, but the lower-paying job seemed to have more potential. He preferred one company, but he really felt a closer bond to his potential supervisor at the other company. He was really struggling with his decision, so he called Steve for one final piece of advice.

Laura suggested that Jamie come to Steve's office immediately since Steve was leaving for vacation tomorrow.

Steve happened to be crossing the bank lobby as Jamie walked in. "Hey Jamie, I was just thinking about you. Come on in here and give me the scoop on your job search."

Jamie had grown very close to Steve during their time together. He told Steve about his job offers and the tough decision he was facing.

"Jamie, you have done a fantastic job. You focused your career search, prepared perfectly and you've secured excellent offers from outstanding companies. The decision you're facing is completely personal and, frankly, I don't think you can make a wrong decision.

Steve hesitated for a moment. "I do have one final question for you, though."

"Ask me anything, Steve. I could really use your help."

Steve leaned back in his chair and smiled. "Jamie, what if you had one more job offer to add to the mix?"

"Steve, I don't think I could handle another job offer right now. I'm about as confused as I can be and another offer will just make matters worse."

"Well, Jamie. What if I told you that I would like to offer you a position right here at Premier Bank?"

Jamie was stunned. He never dreamed that Steve and the bank would be interested in him. "What type of position do you have in mind?"

"We have been looking for the right person to head up a new Small Business Banking division. You will meet with small business owners throughout our region to really understand their needs. Then, you will work with a team of bankers to develop products and services for these important clients and potential clients.

Your involvement in the community will be critical and this will include serving as liaison to the university. You will report directly to me."

Jamie couldn't believe what he was hearing. "Steve, wouldn't you want to hire a banker with experience for this type of position?"

"We thought so, Jamie. I've visited with several local bankers, but none of them have your potential. I believe we can train you to become one of the premier community bankers in the state. I think we'll make a great team."

Steve handed Jamie an envelope with the details of the offer enclosed. "Jamie, I've been debating about whether or not to give this to you because I didn't want to impact your job search and take advantage of our friendship. Please feel free to take all the time you need in considering this offer and you're not going to hurt my feelings if you don't accept it."

Jamie tried to keep his composure, but he was overwhelmed with emotion. After reviewing Steve's generous offer, Jamie was convinced.

"Steve, I would be honored to join your team."

Life Lesson #7

*Success is where opportunity
meets preparation.*

*Never worry, always maintain a
positive attitude and focus only
on things you
can control.*

*Everything else will
take care of itself.*

Out of the Blocks

Jamie's career with Premier Bank started much differently than he had imagined. Instead of being the center of attention he was accustomed to in college, he was largely ignored. It wasn't that his co-workers acted inappropriately toward him or consciously ignored him. They were just focused on their own jobs.

Jamie also faced a significant learning curve. As Jamie expected, much of the training necessary to be a banker wasn't learned in a classroom, it was learned on the job. He just wasn't prepared for everything he would need to learn in order to be a productive employee.

First, he had to learn the basics. He had to learn where to park, where the bathrooms and copier machine were located, how to use the computer and phone system, everyone's name and position, how to order office supplies, and many other important, but mundane, details.

He also had to master certain job-specific information. Jamie had to learn the bank's history, hours, products and services. He had to learn the bank's core operating system, market position, and the unique industry vocabulary that bankers use on a daily basis. In his early days, Jamie nodded and smiled his way through many office conversations that he did not understand.

The most challenging part of Jamie's new job, however, proved to be developing relationships with his coworkers. Jamie realized very early that 'selling' himself to his fellow employees by sharing his collegiate accomplishments and resume' simply did not work.

Jamie's coworkers weren't interested in his resume' or past accomplishments. They were interested in him and how he contributed to the company. Jamie had to 'de-program' his campus climber mentality and become a more genuine, caring person. He had to earn their respect each and every day. He was always the first to arrive at the office and the last to leave.

Jamie also had to earn his coworkers trust. The more he cared about them and carried his weight as a team member, the more they liked him. Jamie invited a different coworker to lunch every day, and he truly enjoyed getting to know them. He was always honest and never took credit for others' achievements.

Jamie also began to understand the value of experience. The employees he worked with had been in the banking industry for years and everything seemed so easy for them. He began to realize that everyone at Premier Bank was on the same team and he started asking for advice and direction. It was amazing how helpful his coworkers would be when he would ask for their advice.

Jamie realized the same held true for his community involvement. It took a minimum of two to three years of consistent attendance and involvement for his fellow civic leaders to get to know him and realize that his motives were pure. As Steve once told him, "Jamie, it takes a year to prove you'll show up, a year to prove your worth, and in the third year, you'll start building strong relationships and getting some business." Jamie saw others try to sell their products before developing this trust and it backfired virtually every time.

Over time, Jamie began to earn the trust and respect of his peers. His creativity and interpersonal skills brought value to the company and community while his work ethic was never questioned. He received his first promotion and was well on his way to a successful, long-term career with Premier Bank.

Or so it seemed.

Life Lesson #8

You must earn the respect and trust of any team before you can lead them.

You earn this respect and trust by being honest, working hard, following through on your commitments, listening well and genuinely caring about your team members.

.

Gaining Stride

Jamie focused intently on developing the critical skills that Steve taught him during his career search. Over the next few years, Jamie became a significant contributor to Premier Bank's success. His reputation as a knowledgeable, innovative banker began to spread throughout the community and ultimately, the entire region.

He loved his career and became involved in numerous community organizations including the Chamber of Commerce, Rotary Club and Ambassadors Committee.

His network of contacts began to grow and so did his professional opportunities. Other banks began to realize that Jamie would be an asset for their organizations. He was approached by competitors on several occasions.

Jamie was now married with two small children. His wife stayed at home with the children and, while he loved that she stayed at home, one income definitely made for a tight budget.

Jamie ignored the initial job inquiries from other firms because of his loyalty to Steve and his love for the employees at Premier, but eventually he became restless. Suddenly, he began to feel underappreciated. Was he being paid enough? Why was Steve always getting all of the attention? Why didn't he have more responsibility? Would he ever have the opportunity to be president of Premier Bank?

Ultimately, his new-found frustration led to a job interview and, eventually, a significant job offer. He was a Vice President at Premier Bank and he was offered the position of Senior Vice President at a major competitor. The new position included additional management responsibility and a 20% pay raise.

Jamie thought about the new position for several days. It seemed as if other bankers moved up by changing banks, but there was always risk in any move. How would he face Steve and his co-workers in the community? What if he decided to stay at Premier? Would staying show his loyalty and be rewarded, or would it be a career limiting move? Would Steve be disappointed in him for even considering another opportunity? Steve had done so much for Jamie, but even he made three moves prior to his current position. Finally, Jamie decided to set an appointment to visit with Steve.

"Good morning Jamie. How are things in your world?" Steve was always such a nice guy and this made Jamie's announcement even tougher.

"I'm doing okay Steve, but I think we need to talk. I have a substantial job offer and I really need your advice."

"Congratulations Jamie, I knew this would happen sooner or later. You are just too talented not to be sought after. Tell me about your offer, but don't expect me to be objective in my advice. I definitely don't want to lose you."

Jamie told Steve about the position and the struggle he'd been having with the decision. "Steve, I appreciate everything you've done for me and I want to be loyal to you. I also need to make the career move that is best for me and my family. What should I do?"

"Jamie, these are tough decisions. I believe you have a very bright future here at Premier, but you need to make the best decision for you. Job moves are risky and you need to make sure you know everything you can about your potential employer. You don't want any surprises."

"Steve, it's not possible to know everything about a potential employer. You made a couple of career moves. How did they work out for you?"

"One worked well and the other did not. My first move was excellent. I fit into my new bank's culture perfectly and my skill set was exactly what they needed. We were immensely successful and the bank ultimately sold, leading to my second major opportunity.

I wasn't quite as fortunate during the second move. I became enamored by a great title and compensation package and I failed to thoroughly analyze the company or ask the right questions. I did not fit well into the company's culture and did not have a shared vision with owners. That move could have been disastrous, but, fortunately, the owners here at Premier Bank offered me this position, which has turned out very well.

Jamie, it's extremely difficult for an employee to find the perfect fit. You can love the organization and struggle with your supervisor. You can love your supervisor, but struggle with the organization. You can ask all the right questions and still make a mistake. Above all, always remember that no job is perfect. They all have positives and negatives, and you just have to make sure the positives outweigh the negatives.

Jamie agreed. "I understand that Steve, but I've also watched employees get passed over because their employer takes them for granted. You are certainly not doing this, but how can I make sure it doesn't happen to me?"

"I don't think you can ever be too loyal, Jamie, but I do think it is important to properly manage your career. All salaries, unless you or your family happen to own the company, are set by the market. How much does your employer have to pay to keep you? Often, students think you can 'kiss up' to the boss to get a higher salary, but the boss's job is to increase profits and decrease costs. Your boss will give you a significant salary adjustment when he believes it will cost him more to replace you.

You can never allow yourself to be taken for granted by your employer. Keep your ear to the ground and occasionally test the market. An offer from another company is really the best way to determine your market value, but you should only attempt to leverage a competitor's offer if you are a valuable asset to your company and prepared to take the job offer if your employer doesn't counter.

Sometimes this strategy can backfire. I have seen people attempt to leverage offers without following these two rules, and this can be disastrous. You also have to be very careful how you communicate your job offer to your employer. You never want to create bad feelings or burn bridges with a former employer. The world is very small and you never know when you might cross paths again.

Jamie, I can't tell you what decision to make, but I can make it easier for you to stay here. You have proven yourself as a valuable member of our team, and we definitely want to keep you. Due to the increased risk of making a move, I don't feel like I need to match them, but I will certainly get your salary close to the one they're offering you."

Steve took the time to visit with Jamie about the future of Premier Bank and how Jamie would fit into the bank's long-term plan. Although Steve was young and Jamie knew he would be the CEO for several years, he was encouraged by the opportunity for expanded responsibility and influence within the company.

Steve suggested that Jamie should consider returning to college for his Masters of Business Administration degree. "Jamie, an MBA helps you to develop a stronger background in all areas of the company from marketing to management to accounting and much more. I think it would be a great next step for you. ITU has a fantastic night program that wouldn't interfere with your work, but you'd better talk with your wife about it first."

After their conversation, Jamie decided to stay with Steve and Premier Bank. He felt that Steve's counteroffer was fair and realized that perhaps the grass isn't always greener on the other side.

Jamie was relieved to have this decision behind him and looked forward to his future at Premier Bank.

Life Lesson #9

It's important to manage your career and never allow your employer to take you for granted.

Your salary is determined by your value within the market.

A legitimate job offer is a great way to determine your market value, but you must be willing to accept the offer before you present it to your current company.

The Home Stretch

Jamie grew into a great banker, family man, church and civic leader. He consistently set challenging goals and held himself accountable for those goals each and every day.

Jamie's wife supported him in his effort to get his MBA. It was challenging and, at times, Jamie just didn't think he could get it all done. But, in the end, he graduated right on time.

As a banker, Jamie was always fair and responsive. He provided his customers with tremendous service but always protected the bank as well. Jamie became an excellent manager and was known as a good listener and team player who always put his employees first.

He was a caring father and a thoughtful, dependable husband. Although other careers promised a higher level of compensation, his position gave him the flexibility to attend his children's events and make it home at a decent time each night to see his wife. Jamie always tried to put his family first.

Jamie was also well-respected throughout the community. He gave selflessly of his time, resources and talents, as long as it didn't interfere with his family. He also became a leader in his church and was a trusted advisor to many. He never sought the spotlight, but increasingly, it seemed that leadership opportunities found him.

Eventually, Jamie worked his way up to Executive Vice President at Premier Bank and became a confidante and partner to Steve Patrick. The bank continued to grow and soon became known as the top community bank in Illinois.

Although circumstances were not always perfect, Jamie always remembered the words that Steve Patrick told him years earlier. "Jamie, the real world is a marathon and not a sprint. No one is keeping score but you. If you can get up in the morning, say your prayers at night, and feel good about yourself, consider yourself a success. Don't get caught up in what society thinks about you or you'll never be content.

Always be honest and work hard. Give the credit to others and never search for the spotlight. Life is about much more than who can accumulate the most stuff and make the most headlines."

Sometimes Jamie was tempted to cut corners or take credit for others' achievements. Occasionally, he became frustrated that he didn't move up in the organization fast enough. Every once in awhile, he began working too many hours and taking his family for granted, but the words of Steve Patrick always rang in his head and centered him.

Then, late one Friday afternoon, Steve walked into Jamie's office. "Jamie, you have served me and Premier Bank well for many years. I trust you and appreciate your dedication. I have decided to retire and the Board of Directors has unanimously selected you to serve as the bank's new President & Chief Executive Officer."

Tears welled up in Jamie's eyes. "Steve, this is a dream come true. You have been such a friend and mentor to me. I certainly hate to see you retire, but I would be honored to succeed you."

Life Lesson #10

Life is a marathon and not a sprint. Don't get caught up in what society thinks. No one is keeping score but you.

Be honest and work hard. Give the credit to others and never search for the spotlight.

Life is about much more than who can accumulate the most stuff.

The Finish Line

One sunny spring afternoon, as Jamie was enjoying a round of golf with three of his executive officers, his cell phone rang. It was Laura, his assistant.

"Jamie, we just received a call from the hospital and the news is not good. Chairman Steve Patrick had a massive heart attack."

Jamie dropped everything and drove to the hospital as fast as he could. Steve had a minor scare with his heart two or three years earlier, but this time it sounded much more severe.

As he was driving, Jamie thought about his first meeting with Steve Patrick almost twenty-five years ago when he was just a student. He remembered his excitement when Steve offered him his first job.

He thought about the hours they spent talking and sharing their innermost thoughts with each other. He loved visiting with Steve about their lives, their families, and their dreams. Steve always took the time to talk with him, even when Jamie knew he didn't have the time.

Jamie soon arrived at the hospital. As he walked into Steve's room, Jamie could tell that something was wrong. Steve was pale and looked very tired.

Steve's wife Jan was standing beside his bed. She gave Jamie a big hug and welcomed him into the room. "Jamie, I'm so glad you made it. Steve's been asking for you."

Jamie didn't know what to say. "Steve and Jan, I am so sorry. I came as soon as I heard."

Steve could barely speak. "Jamie, I may not make it through this one, but I wanted to share one last life lesson with you."
"I would love nothing more, Steve."

"Jamie, when you are in my situation, you begin to realize what is really important. As I was riding in the ambulance to the hospital, it occurred to me that one word sums up the ideal life on this earth."

"What is that word, Steve?"

"It's a word that you taught me years ago when we first met. The key to life in this world is balance. If a person can achieve balance in this life, he has achieved everything."

"What do you mean?" Jamie couldn't recall teaching Steve any life lessons.

Steve struggled to talk. "Jamie, many people tend to place too much emphasis on one area of their lives and forget about the others.

Executives spend all of their time and energy at work. They achieve personal wealth at the expense of their families. So, they live a lonely, meaningless existence surrounded by their material possessions.

It's also difficult to live a fulfilling life when you are always worried about your financial situation. So, you can't focus exclusively on your family and fail to meet your financial obligations. Motivation and achieving goals is a wonderful thing, as long as you don't neglect your family and friends.

Most importantly, we must prioritize our spiritual life correctly. I believe, like you, that our life here on earth is merely preparation for our eternal life. Placing too much emphasis on earthly possessions with no focus on our spiritual life is the biggest mistake of all.

Jamie, never allow your career to dominate your entire life. I can tell you that the old saying is true, when you are in a situation like this, your only wish is for more time with the people you love. I certainly don't wish that I'd spent more time at the office."

Jamie understood exactly what Steve was saying. "Steve, thank you so much for this final lesson. I only hope that I can achieve the life balance you have achieved."

The doctor entered the room and asked Jamie to step outside. Before he left, Jamie gave his old friend one last goodbye.

A tear fell down Steve's cheek. "Jamie, I couldn't be prouder of you. I'll see you real soon."

Life Lesson #11

*The key to a fulfilling
life is balance.*

*Strive for balance in your
spiritual, personal and
professional life.*

*Focusing too much on one area
at the exclusion of the others
will lead to a life filled with
frustration and disappointment.*

Full Circle

Five years had gone by since Steve's funeral and Jamie thought about him each and every day. They were not only business partners but best friends as well. They had survived two recessions, a real estate crisis and their children's teenage years together. Through thick and thin, they were always there for each other.

Jamie continued Steve's legacy and made Premier Bank even stronger. Premier continued its tremendous growth and even stronger financial performance. Jamie's selfless attitude created unmatched employee loyalty and a warm, nurturing corporate culture.

As Jamie inched closer to retirement, he couldn't help but reflect on his life and all of the wonderful opportunities he had been given. He glanced around his office at the various awards and certificates. Citizen of the Year, Top Performing Bank, Chamber of Commerce President, Outstanding Alumni Award and many more. Steve was correct, the trophies really didn't mean much, but the memories and accomplishments that went with them certainly did.

He stared at the picture of his beautiful family. It seemed impossible that he had been married for almost 30 years and his oldest daughter would soon be getting married. It seemed like only yesterday when he held her in the hospital nursery.

Jamie thought back to that cold November day when he first met Steve Patrick. That meeting changed Jamie's life forever. He had been blessed with a wonderful life.

Suddenly, Jamie's daydreaming was interrupted by an intercom call from Laura. "Jamie, it is Dr. Gary Williams from ITU's College of Business."

Jamie picked up the phone. "Good afternoon, Dean Williams. How are things at ITU today?"

"Not bad at all, Jamie. Thank you for asking. Jamie, I know you are very busy, but I have a favor to ask of you.

I just finished meeting with an outstanding young man who is really struggling to make the right career decision and I think you could help him a great deal. Would you mind meeting with him?"

Jamie smiled as tears came to his eyes. "I would love to meet with him, Dr. Edwards. Many years ago, I promised a good friend of mine that I would always help if given the opportunity. Please have him give me a call. I may have a few life lessons to share with him."

Life Lesson #12

*Always give of your time
and resources.*

*You make a living out of what
you get.*

*You make a life out of what
you give.*

-Winston Churchill

Bonus Material:

18 ways to get ahead in your new job!

As Jamie taught us, landing your first job is only half the battle. After you've survived orientation, learned where the restroom and copy machines are, and figured out how to check your voice mail, the real work (literally) begins.

How can you excel and advance in your new organization while maintaining the respect of your peers? Following are 18 ways to get ahead in your new job. These tips became very popular in the college classes I taught and I hope you enjoy them too!

1. **Always practice the Golden Rule.** Treating others the way you wish to be treated will guarantee your future success. Whether you are interacting with your supervisor, coworkers, clients or competitors, always treat them the way you would want to be treated if you were in their shoes. Would you want a subordinate who is always late or misses deadlines? Would you want a peer who takes all the credit? Would you want a husband who always puts work first? You get the picture.

2. **Arrive at work five minutes before your boss and leave work five minutes after her.** As far as the boss knows, you could have been working all night! Very powerful subconscious message.

3. **When asked a question in meetings, always contemplate your answer before blurting it out.** Thoughtful consideration gives you the appearance of being more cerebral and 'deeper' than your coworkers.

4. **Always invite someone to lunch and never go by yourself.** This allows you to not only appear popular, but also develop great relationship with

coworkers. Never spend your lunch gossiping about work. Always ask questions of your lunch guest and find out as much about him as you can. This helps you to develop a reputation as a good listener and a caring person, both very positive attributes.

5. **Always be polite yet persistent.** It is important to be respected and liked by your peers and superiors, but you can't be so nice that you are a pushover. You must have a certain toughness and persistence to succeed, particularly as you advance into senior management positions. Polite yet persistent is a great rule to use.

6. **Occasionally, take some paperwork and reading home with you at night.** You must be careful not to let your work impact your personal life, but doing a little reading right after dinner or before bed should be harmless and can allow you to stay ahead of the curve and up to date on industry issues. Carrying paperwork home at night also makes you look like an overachiever to your boss!

7. **Try to send e-mails before and after work, and copy the boss when it is appropriate.** You don't want to force this one or your motives

will become obvious, but if done correctly, this tip makes you look like the consummate hard worker and overachiever.

8. **When you reach the level of supervisor, send regular e-mails bragging on your employees to everyone, and be sure to copy your boss.** This one is a gem. Sending complimentary e-mails to everyone and including your boss has three very positive effects. It creates loyalty among your employees because you are selflessly promoting them. It impresses your boss because it highlights that you are a great manager with good employees. And, it let's your boss know that you are a team player who puts his employees first.

The key is to focus on very specific and deserving employee compliments or this tip can appear insincere. If done correctly, this strategy is money in the bank!

9. **Always dress for your boss's job, but don't go overboard.** Dressing for the job you want really does work because it helps the boss picture you in the new role; however, if you take it too far and overdress, you will appear out of touch and desperate.

10. **Wear thin socks (guys).** This one ties closely with #9. Nothing says amateur like wooly dress socks that fall down around your shoes, particularly when you cross your legs in a meeting.

11. **Host as many meetings as you can, and always command the dry-erase board.** Nothing says power like an individual writing on a dry-erase board. Just make sure the meetings are necessary and productive.

12. **Use larger words than necessary without seeming too ridiculous.** Example: "My perception is" instead of "I think". A large vocabulary shows intellectual strength, but it can make you look silly if overdone.

13. **Forward your boss newspaper clippings or online articles that he would enjoy.** Another really strong tip. This shows the boss you are interested in more than just your job, you are plugged in to current events, and you are upwardly mobile.

14. **Send personalized birthday cards to immediate superiors, coworkers and special clients, and send handwritten thank you**

notes as appropriate. These tips help you to develop strong personal connections with those professional relationships that matter most to you. Did you know what virtually all United States Presidents actively wrote thank you notes?

15. **Never stand around talking socially with coworkers.** Always have these 'meetings' on the phone or in your office and make them look businesslike. Nothing says 'I'm unnecessary' like gawking and chatting on company time. A definite career killer.

16. **To experience true job security, learn to create revenue.** Companies (and bosses) live and die by their ability to create profits and, by definition, you can't be profitable if you don't have revenue.   You will find that the most secure person within a company is always the 'rainmaker' whose relationships and skills result in revenue for the company.

17. **Be an active listener.** When the boss is speaking to your group, he notices the reactions he receives. If you listen closely and appear supportive to him, he will remember you. Active listening is a great way to differentiate yourself from a large group.

18. Maintain a good attitude at all times. You must consistently be in a good mood. Never treat your clients or coworkers with disrespect and never allow problems at home to show up at work. Your bad attitude or moodiness will impact employee morale and ensure your early departure from the company.

<u>Do You Want More Out of the Blocks?</u>

We hope you enjoyed Out of the Blocks! Please visit www.outoftheblocks.net for the following:

o *Subscribe to Kouplen's monthly Out of the Blocks e-newsletter*

o *Participate in the Out of the Blocks blog*

o *Order additional copies of Out of the Blocks*

o *Contact Kouplen about speaking to your college or high school student group*

About the Author

Sean Kouplen has been a bank president and owner, Chamber of Commerce President, National Alumni president, an award-winning professor, founder of a thriving community church, and Citizen of the Year in his hometown….all by the age of 34.

Kouplen's real passion, however, is to helping individuals live a fulfilling life by creating a clear vision for their future, and developing and implementing a plan to achieve their vision.

Kouplen developed this passion while serving as an adjunct professor for Oklahoma State University. While teaching there, he was continuously interrogated by students, both young and old, who were concerned and confused about their future.

Out of the Blocks is Kouplen's attempt to help these individuals, and millions like them, achieve the success they deserve.

Kouplen is currently CEO of Regent Bank, and is a sought-after speaker for student and young professional groups throughout the nation. He enjoys reading, playing golf, ranching with his father, and spending time with his wife Angela and their two daughters, Emory and Kennedy.

To learn more about Sean Kouplen, visit www. outoftheblocks.net

1509942

Made in the USA